Christian Kimmich, Hannah Janetschek, Lutz Meyer-Ohlendorf, Jennifer Meyer-Ueding, Julian Sagebiel, Fritz Reusswig, Kai Rommel, Markus Hanisch

Methods for Stakeholder Analysis

Exploring actor constellations in transition and change processes towards sustainable resource use and the case of Hyderabad, India

Emerging megacities
Discussion Papers
Edited by Konrad Hagedorn, Christine Werthmann, Dimitrios Zikos, Ramesh Chennamaneni

Humboldt-Universität zu Berlin
Department of Agricultural Economics
Division of Resource Economics
Philippstr. 13, House 12
10115 Berlin

Tel.: +49 (0)30 2093 6305
Fax: +49 (0)30 2093 6497
www.agrar.hu-berlin.de/struktur/institute/wisola/fg/ress
www.sustainable-hyderabad.de/emerging-megacities

Contact: emerging.megacities@hu-berlin.de

The Emerging megacities Discussion Papers are available at:
www.eh-verlag.de

ISSN print edition 2193-6927

Emerging megacities Discussion Papers are prepared by researchers working on topics in the realm of sustainable development in Megacities of Tomorrow, a research priority by the German Ministry of Education and Research (BMBF). The papers have been peer-reviewed by a board of external reviewers.
Views and opinions expressed do not necessarily represent those of the Division of Resource Economics.
Comments are highly welcome and should be sent directly to the authors.
We welcome contributions on any topics related to Megacities of Tomorrow. Further information on the submission procedure is given at:
www.sustainable-hyderabad.de/emerging-megacities

Kimmich, Christian; Janetschek, Hannah; Meyer-Ohlendorf, Lutz; Meyer-Ueding, Jennifer; Sagebiel, Julian; Reusswig, Fritz; Rommel, Kai; Hanisch, Markus

Methods for Stakeholder Analysis
Exploring actor constellations in transition and change processes towards sustainable resource use and the case of Hyderabad, India

Emerging megacities Discussion Papers, Volume 1/2009

ISBN/EAN: 978-3-86741-780-8
First published in 2012 by Europaeischer Hochschulverlag GmbH & Co KG, Bremen, Germany.

© Europaeischer Hochschulverlag GmbH & Co KG, Fahrenheitstr. 1, D-28359 Bremen (www.eh-verlag.de). All rights reserved.

Cover: Photo "Metropolis", ferendus (flickr). Creative Commons License

No part of this publication may be reproduced or transmitted, in any form or by any means, electronic, mechanical, photocopying, recording or otherwise, or stored in any retrieval system of nay nature, without the written permission of the copyright holder and the publisher, application for which shall be made to the publisher.

Methods for Stakeholder Analysis

Exploring actor constellations in transition and change processes towards sustainable resource use and the case of Hyderabad, India

Christian Kimmich[*,†] *Hannah Janetschek*[†] *Lutz Meyer-Ohlendorf*[‡] *Jennifer Meyer-Ueding*[§] *Julian Sagebiel*[§] *Fritz Reusswig*[‡] *Kai Rommel*[†] *Markus Hanisch*[§]

May 2009

Abstract

This contribution depicts a stakeholder analysis process that is being conducted within a R&D project in Hyderabad focusing on energy, resources and climate in a transformation process of lifestyles, co-operation and governance structures. The paper starts with a brief review of research on theories and methods for stakeholder analysis from a range of theoretical backgrounds including project and natural resource management. We depict a specific conceptual framework and methods for natural resource governance and relate this approach to the case of Hyderabad as a multilayered emerging megacity with a multiplicity of organisations and interrelated networks. We derive an operational guideline with methods for stakeholder identification and mapping and typologies for differentiation and categorisation of stakeholders. The differentiation is led by attributes such as objectives, interests, organisational structure, incentives, power and resources as well as interdependencies and relations between stakeholders. Empirical data has been gathered from website profiles, judicial sources such as acts and orders, public discourses in newspapers, surveys and semi-structured interviews. The empirical findings indicate that given the strong nexus between climate, energy and resource use and the comprehensive approach of the respective project, a broad spectrum of stakeholders had to be taken into consideration. Depending on one of the three major approaches, lifestyles, cooperation and governance structures, a different set of stakeholders can be defined as primary. The findings serve for multi-stakeholder participation planning processes in research and development.

Key words: *stakeholder analysis, urban transformation, natural resource, lifestyles, governance structure, climate change, Hyderabad, India*

---

[*] Corresponding author. Tel.: +49 30 2093 6430. Email: christian.kimmich@staff.hu-berlin.de
[†] Division of Resource Economics, Humboldt Universität zu Berlin, Philippstraße 13, 10115 Berlin
[‡] Potsdam Institute for Climate Impact Research, P.O. Box 60 12 03, 14412 Potsdam
[§] Berlin Institute for Co-operative Studies, Humboldt Universität zu Berlin, Luisenstraße 53, 10117 Berlin

1 Introduction

Societies have become increasingly differentiated. At the same time, perception of what a society is composed of has undergone tremendous change. The notions of networks and governance clearly state this change, where networks might become even more important "than markets and hierarchies" (Powell 1991). What have once been households, firms and a state is now a composition of interconnected units covering several household strata, small to multinational enterprises, civil society organisations, industry associations, ministries, media, etc. Stakeholder analysis contributes to this differentiated perception of societies. The research & development project in Hyderabad striving towards an urban transformation accounting for sustainable resource use and therewith the mitigation of and adaptation to climate change has to incorporate Hyderabad's complex society as a whole. A less holistic approach would not be able to cope with the aim to induce transformation in Hyderabad in a sustainable way. Certainly all parts of the city's society can be regarded as acting subjects and affected objects in the fields of climate change and energy use. Our guiding research questions within this contribution are hence: Who can be *identified* as a concrete stakeholder[1]? Which parts of the society play a *crucial role* as they induce change within this transformation process?

The R&D project in Hyderabad this stakeholder analysis is part of, includes a multifaceted approach towards sustainable natural resource use. Three major approaches with a threefold, interrelated stakeholder analysis can be distinguished: (1) The first approach marks lifestyles as drivers of social change and aims towards lifestyle changes for sustainability transition (Reusswig et al. 2003; Sudarshan 2008). The stakeholders that shape public discourses, such as the media, play a crucial role within this approach (Reusswig et al. 2009a). (2) The second approach focuses on co-operation and self-governance of small-scale enterprises and private households towards climate change mitigation and a low-energy path. At the centre of this approach, these small-scale enterprises and private households are the primary stakeholders and are linked to a spectrum of related stake-

---

[1] The term "stakeholder" has become ubiquitously used for summarising actors that are related to an issue, organisation or project. The model can refer to individuals, parties, groups, networks, associations and organisations that have an influence on, affect or are affected Freeman. 1984: 46 by the issue at stake, the pivotal actor, organisation or project. This is probably the broadest definition of who could be a stakeholder (Mitchell et al. 1997). Typical definitions *referring to an organisation* include those who have an influence on the organisation's strategy (Nutt and Backoff. 1992: 439), the fability "to place a claim on the organisation's attention, resources, or output" (Bryson 1995: 27 cited in Bryson 2004), "the power to respond to, negotiate with, and change the strategic future of the organisation" (Eden and Ackermann. 1998: 117) and the interdependency of stakeholders' and the organisation's goals (Johnson and Scholes 2002: 206 cited in Bryson 2004).

holders (Hanisch et al. 2009). (3) The third approach focuses on institutions and related governance structures for sustainable resource use, where governmental stakeholders and interest groups of private organisations play an important role in shaping policies (Kimmich et al. 2009). Depending on the approach, a different spectrum of stakeholders has to be chosen. Nevertheless, the approaches for identifying and analysing stakeholders can be based on a common method set.

The project's stakeholder analysis can revert to a vast variety of scientific contributions. The different emphases on how stakeholder analyses can be conceptualised have been brought forward mainly by areas such as corporate, public and natural resource management research as well as project and development studies. The origination in business management had an influential impact on concepts in the other areas (Reed et al. 2009). Later, their increasing differentiation raised important new aspects. In natural resource management, a distinction between active (affecting) and passive (affected) stakeholders became common (Grimble and Wellard 1997). The interdependence of actors, created through the physical properties of transactions is highlighted in institutional resource economics (Hagedorn 2008). Especially relevant in public management, where creating public value and advancing a common good are elementary objectives is an inclusive approach that emphasises the importance to include powerless and unorganised stakeholders (Bryson 2004). The methodology described in this paper draws on this variety, but with a special focus on concepts that have evolved with relation to natural resources.

This contribution is organised as follows: First, we review the literature, derive and explain stages of stakeholder analysis with respective common methods and in Chapter 2 focus on how to make the stakeholder analysis operational and instrumental within a research & development project. In Chapter 3 we then exemplify our chosen method set with first results of the case of a R&D project for sustainable natural resource use in an urban environment in Hyderabad. Finally, we synthesise empirical results and draw some conclusions for stakeholder analyses in the given context in Chapter 4.

2 Stakeholder analysis for transition and change processes

The project's goal is not only to describe and analyse the *transition process* ('research') but to induce *change processes* ('development') and to find out, which stakeholders are most relevant for this purpose. This distinction is paralleled by a common differentiation made in respective literature concerning the rationale of a stakeholder analysis (see for example Reed et al. 2009): (1) *Descriptive approaches* have a phenomenological orientation and look at the stakeholders and their interrelations emphasising a grounded empirical basis. They mainly identify and describe characteristics of stakeholders and often serve as inputs for normative and instrumental approaches. Heuristics, such as the stakeholder mapping methods can be used for this purpose, also relating the pivotal organisation or project to its stakeholders. (2) *Normative stakeholder approaches* assume that understanding the different perspectives and conflicting interests of the stakeholders is crucial and an environment of 'intersubjective validation' is necessary to induce change towards sustainability . The stakeholder analysis can contribute to this communication process. (3) *Instrumental stakeholder approaches* focus on pursuing the organisation's or project's objectives. The analysis identifies, how stakeholders are related to these objectives and aims at a strategic management of stakeholder relations. In natural resource management, instrumental stakeholder analyses are used to surmount obstacles in adopting new technologies and adapting technologies to target groups (Johnson 2004 cited in Reed et al. 2009). *Normative* justifications in stakeholder dialogues through stakeholder analyses can be *instrumental* to achieve outcomes. This approach can increase participation and involvement, transform relationships, increase trust and finally lead to ownership of the processes in accordance with the objectives. (Reed et al. 2009) The level of participation that is aimed at also implies which methods are most useful to apply in a stakeholder analysis[2]. Reed et al (2009) offer a good overview evaluating their participation level, strengths and weaknesses and resources required.

Typically, a distinction of three stages of stakeholder analysis can be derived from theories and approaches comprising (1) the identification of stakeholders, (2) the differentiation and categorisation and (3) the analysis of relations between stakeholders. These stages with their respective methods will be explained in the following sub-chapters.

2.1 Stakeholder identification: Who has a stake in urban transformation towards sustainability?

In order to prevent the exclusion of potential stakeholders at this stage, the identification process is best conducted on a rather descriptive basis using the broadest definition of stakeholders. A project with the objective of creating public value implies a more inclusive perspective while in a corporate management context focusing on the effective

---

[2] A range of available methods includes focus groups, stakeholder-led categorisation of stakeholders, semi-structured interviews or social network analyses. Reed et al. 2009: 1937

achievement of private goals only a selection of the most likely affecting stakeholders is relevant. However, a boundary has to be drawn at some stage in order to keep the process operational.

Drawing the boundaries for stakeholder analysis is crucial yet difficult to realise with analytical tools that use geographical boundaries.[3] An analytical approach that has been developed in the field of institutional resource economics focuses on the physical side of the transactions that the project's objective is aiming at. The "Institutions of Sustainability" framework (IoS) (Hagedorn et al. 2002; Hagedorn 2008) relates actors and transactions[4] with the respective institutions and governance structures. Through the choices and consecutive actions of actors, physical and institutional transactions are realised that can have a multiplicity of intended and unintended[5] outcomes depending on the transactions' characteristics, e.g. their modularity and decomposability. Through the outcomes, transactions create interdependency and force interaction. Transactions have both physical properties and an institutional side. Through a focus on the physical side of transactions, the involved actors and their interdependency can be analytically identified. The degree of interdependency can be derived both from the physical as well as from the institutional side, e.g. the amount of energy that comes with a transaction and the respective price that is paid or the degree of emission of a power plant and the differentiation of respective law. This can help differentiating the stakeholders and their degree of involvement regarding the transaction that is focused upon.

Some methods to identify stakeholders are not based on an analytical concept and yet the most commonly used approaches in stakeholder analysis. This is the case for "snowball sampling", which is the fastest method to start identifying potential stakeholders. Initial stakeholders are interviewed for identifying other stakeholders. Potential stakeholders can also be found through searches in news and on websites that give a quick

---

[3] Drawing geographical lines can be arbitrary, as the case of GHG emissions shows, with an impact on the whole globe. At the same time, by far not all organisations within a geographical region will be identified as stakeholders. A geographical boundary may be useful for stakeholders such as households, but nor for organisations from outside the region who may still influence transition paths.

[4] Transactions can be defined as intentional actions of actors, that change physical or institutional entities or transmit information. The electricity transmission or coal combustion is such an example. Transactions can also be parts of these, such as the feed-in of electricity. These transactions are the unit of analysis within the transaction interdependence cycle (Hagedorn 2008). Interactions can emerge as processes of uncertainty out of transactions, when at least one other actor becomes involved and reacts.

[5] The unintended outcomes of transactions are often defined as negative or positive "external effects" in economics. However, this is only a special case where the actor is generally related to the whole "external environment", "all others" or "the law", i.e. some undifferentiated object. In transaction analyses, a differentiation is being made for the actors that are involved.

overview and even links to other potential stakeholders. "Brainstorming" is another commonly used method that is especially fruitful if conducted within a group that is involved in the issue at stake. All these methods can be enhanced through the involvement of the first identified stakeholders while searching for further stakeholders.

2.2 Typologies and stakeholder relations (analyses at the micro- and meso-level)

Having identified most of the potential stakeholders, we can start to analyse their characteristics. A differentiation and categorisation of stakeholders helps to structure all potential stakeholders and to get an overview and understanding of who might play which role within the project later on. This is also the stage, at which literature on stakeholder analysis provides most methods, typologies, tools and instruments that can be applied. Methods can include surveys, semi-structured interviews and focus groups. Their relative strengths and weaknesses are discussed extensively elsewhere. Reconstructive categorisations aim at avoiding the bias of the researcher through participative categorisation. Both the categories or attributes and the process of categorisation can be realised together with the stakeholders, using a scope of adequate group facilitation methods.

Mitchell et al. (1997) propose three types of attributes, along which stakeholders can be analysed and identified as being salient. Stakeholder salience depends on (a) *power*, based on material, financial or symbolic resources, (b) *legitimacy* as socially accepted behaviour and strategies or authority and (c) *urgency*, as the dynamic part identifying which stakeholder counts first. (Mitchell et al. Oct., 1997) Many analytical categorisations are conducted by relating the objectives to the stakeholders, analysing interests and influences, cooperation and competition, etc. This is often realised by using matrices as tools. So-called 'stakeholder commitment matrices' can be built with a differentiation between passive and active support, neutral relation and passive and active opposition towards the project (Jepsen and Eskerod 2009). A commonly used tool is the interest- or 'influence-versus-power diagram' (Eden and Ackermann 1998). Other attributes for categorisation include bases of power, resources or opposition and support (Bryson 2004). These tools have been used within the R&D project and an example will be given in Chapter 3.

A tool that is based on the knowledge gained through typologies and stakeholder profiles is the power-versus-interest matrix (Eden and Ackermann 1998). Stakeholders can be analysed with respect to two basic questions: (1) Which stakeholders are *powerful* enough to support the project goals? (2) Which stakeholders are *interested* in and committed to the project goals? The dimensions of power and interest can be related for each stakeholder in a two-dimensional matrix[6]. The power dimension involves three forms of power: (1) structural and political power, (2) economic power and (3) network-based power. The interest can be derived from the stakeholder's objectives. Four different groups can be identified: (A) Players, who have both power and are interested in the issues of energy and climate, (B) Subjects, who are interested in the issue but have little power, (C) Context Setters, who have power but are hardly interested in the issue, and (D) The Crowd, neither having power nor being interested in the issue at stake.

Besides helping to determine which players' interests and power bases must be taken into account in order to address the objectives of a project, the analysis of power versus interest is a potent tool to help highlight coalitions to be encouraged or discouraged. Moreover, the power vs. interest grid provides some information on whose changes in interest could make a difference (Bryson 2004: 31)[7].

Analysing stakeholder relationships goes beyond the relation to an organisation's or project's objectives and takes the relations *between* stakeholders as a 'meso-level' into account. This can be crucial to further identify the characteristics of stakeholders such as power that evolves through a central network relation. Actor-linkage matrices, Social Network Analysis (SNA) and knowledge mapping are some of the commonly used tools (Reed et al. 2009). Stakeholder mapping is one of the most applicable methods that allows for a visualisation and efficient communication of stakeholder networks. Furthermore, it can serve as a heuristic instrument to identify important relationships and even to plan further participation, as the case of the lifestyle approach will show (see Chapter 3).

---

[6] The two dimensions are related, but divergent. A stakeholder may well be actively engaged with energy and climate issues in the urban context, but still lacks significant power as compared to others ('subjects'). On the other hand, a lot of structurally powerful actors can be found that would be indispensible for putting forward mitigation and adaptation strategies, yet without seeing them actively engaged in any related activities ('context setters'). These might rank low on their agendas, but without their change of priorities the overall issue cannot be moved ahead. In strategic management, the powerful stakeholders are referred to as actors (Eden and Ackermann 1998: 121).

[7] For an example of an influence/power-versus-importance matrix see the stakeholder analysis conducted by the Administrative Staff College of India (ASCI) within a City Development Strategy (CDS) to improve "service levels particularly to the poor", to "achieve economic growth, poverty reduction and good urban governance" (ASCI 2005: 2) A differentiated frame for the analysis of power is also given. 45 stakeholders were identified and analysed for key interests and for the likely impact of the project towards these interests. On the basis of this stakeholder analysis a stakeholder consultation took place to inform them and secure their commitment. The suggestions and observations provided inputs to develop strategies. (ASCI 2005)

In order to make a project development and implementation process operational, keeping in mind the effectiveness regarding the project type and project objectives as well as the efficiency in respect to available resources, further steps have to be taken into consideration that are part of the normative and instrumental rationale of a stakeholder analysis. Together with understanding each stakeholder's objectives, organisational structure and relation to the project, a categorisation into project partners and primary and secondary stakeholders can be made (Freeman 1984). *Partners* can be defined as key stakeholders with whom cooperation is established, strong interests in collaboration exist or a Memorandum of Understanding has been signed. *Primary stakeholders* are those 'nodal agencies', which play a crucial role to achieve the project's goals. *Secondary stakeholders* do have an influence in the issue at stake, but have either a broader mandate or play an inferior role in achieving the project's goals.

3 Hyderabad: the case of a multilayered, emerging megacity

From the methods reviewed in the preceding chapters, a selection has been drawn and applied in a stakeholder analysis within a R&D project that we currently conduct in Hyderabad. For each of the three approaches, lifestyles, co-operation and institutions, some of the most important results will be described in the following sub-chapters. In order to prevent redundancy, for each approach a different part of the stakeholder analysis is presented.

3.1 Stakeholders for lifestyle changes

If the analysis focuses on lifestyle and consumption there is no particular 'address' in a society. Neither is there a more or less clear cut (economic) sector called 'consumption', nor can we find a limited set of social actors shaping it. Even with respect to private households as an economic sector or aggregated actor, it is necessary to consider the multiple social and structural differences between various households. Consumption has to be understood as a social process, while lifestyle dynamics are its structural driver and its social location. Both are not confined to private household activities, but are part of a wider set of actors and institutional practices. Whoever wants to analyse lifestyle and consumption issues in a structurally meaningful way does in fact have to talk about production and consumption systems; and it is only these systems that will become sustainable—or fail to achieve sustainability (Reusswig et al. 2009a). This is an attempt to embed private households in a wider context by considering institutional aspects as well as influential other actors with the power to directly or indirectly shape the urban consumption process with respect to the overall project goals in a meaningful way.

Our analysis on the climate change discourse reveals that the topic of climate change is a medium to low attention issue for the majority of stakeholders in Hyderabad (as in India in general) (Reusswig et al. 2009b). At the same time, the identified minority of individual or collective actors that actually do rate climate change higher on their agendas have the potential to form a critical mass for socio-ecological change in the city if (1) they improve their cooperation, (2) institutional reforms in the urban space increase their impact, and (3) they manage to align with a still 'silent majority' of stakeholders that by now rate climate change to be of minor relevance. The latter point is based on another key finding of our analyses: Actors with high structural power (based either on political, economic or network power) might be turned into potential 'allies' of a low-carbon strategy, if (1) they can interpret adaptation and mitigation options as new opportunities in their option space, (2) climate issues are more closely linked to sustainability issues, and (3) they perceive institutional reforms and stakeholder involvement as being beneficial for their daily operations.

We have tried to embed the private households in a bigger picture including institutional aspects as well as influential other actors with the power to directly or indirectly shape the urban consumption process with respect to the overall project goals in a meaningful way. We analysed each stakeholder within a table through ratings (1=low; 5=high) given by the researchers' team with respect to the three dimensions of power, the relevance of climate change for the organisation, the actual and potential role for climate change mitigation and adaptation respectively, their interests in the project's fields and their potential role for proposed demonstration and pilot projects and policy advisory. The table provides a comprehensive database that serves as the basis for further promotion of stakeholder participation.

Moreover, the results are the basis for a subsequent power vs. interest mapping that locates stakeholders according to their power by also taking into account common interests with the overall project. This visualisation helps to identify the most appropriate stakeholders for each field of interest, it highlights potential for stakeholder cooperation based on common interests, and—most importantly—it visualises the common interest groups according to their power and their interest with the objectives of the project.

The so gained maps depict a subset of all stakeholders we screened, and focus on those we would like to work with in the near future. Figure 1 illustrates the results gained through the mapping taking into account common interests with the overall project.

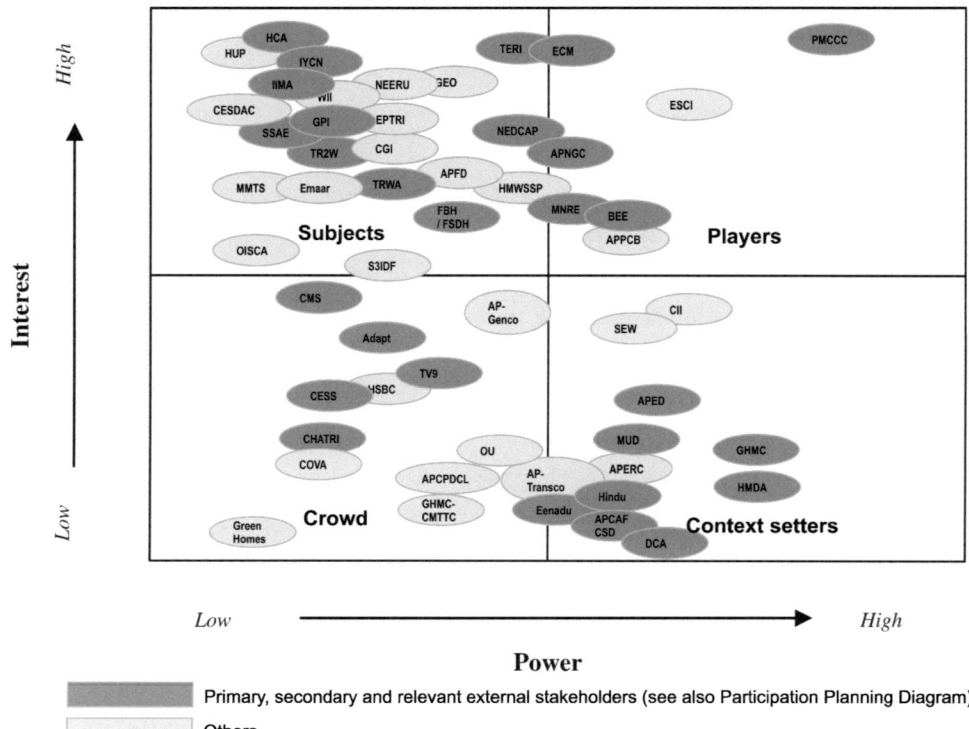

Figure 1: Results of power vs. interest mapping

Source: Based on Bryson (2004: 30)

Based on the foregoing steps a stakeholder map and participation planning diagram was developed (see Figure 2) comprising all the stakeholders that appear functional for any of the project's objectives.

The stakeholder map serves as an approximation to delineate potential participation and cooperation with respect to the project implementation of the lifestyle approach, mediated from the results of the categorisation process.

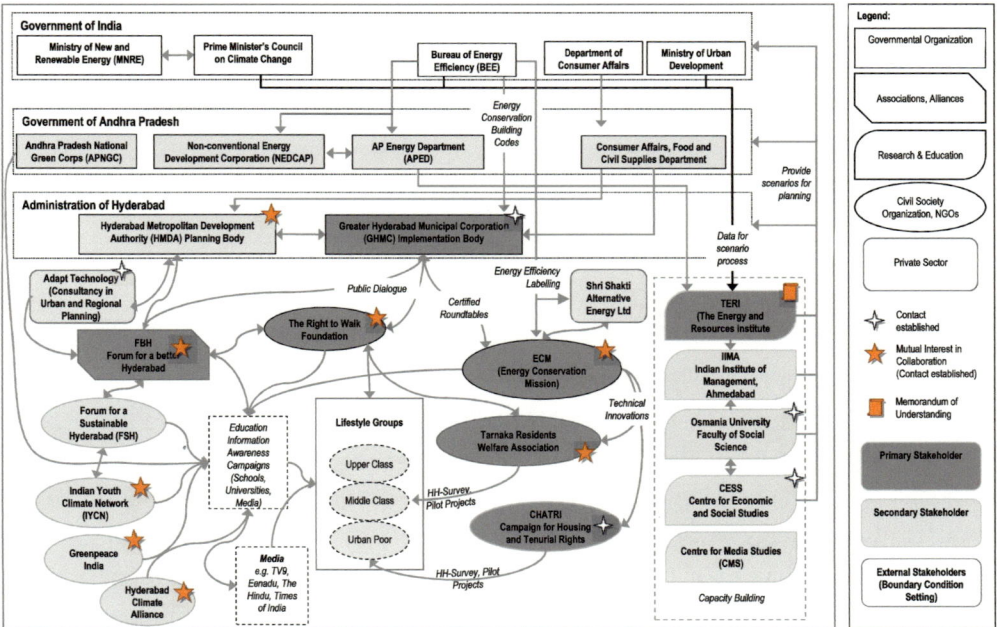

Figure 2: Stakeholder mapping and participation planning diagram
Source: Own draft

3.2 Stakeholders for cooperative self-governance approaches

The cooperative self-governance approach aims at designing cooperative strategies for Kirana shops[8] and small-scale energy consumers to foster their potential contribution towards a sustainable and energy-efficient development of the city of Hyderabad. The cooperative approach is characterised by two particularities shaping the course and the deployment of its stakeholder analysis.

First, the shape of the intended cooperative association(s) is yet to be developed on its primary stakeholders, Kirana retailers and energy consumers in the city, and to be modelled along their characteristics, needs and interests. The decisive step of identifying all relevant stakeholders and their categorisation along the project's objectives as well as the final analysis of their mutual relations in respect to the project will be done subsequently to the process of designing the anticipated Kirana and energy consumer associations. Thus, the emphasis of the stakeholder analysis of this sub-project is

---

[8] Kiranas are traditional Indian mom and pop stores.

- on the Kirana shops, whereas the potential stakeholder groups of supermarkets, suppliers and consumers are analysed in a subsidiary manner and primarily in respect to their relations to Kirana shops as the primary stakeholders.

- on small scale energy consumers whereas potential stakeholder groups of existing cooperative associations (e.g. residents welfare associations, industrial federations) are analysed as potential starting points of the intended energy consumer cooperatives.

Second, the cooperative self-governance approach is largely confined to the local level and encompasses large groups of stakeholders but does not directly pertain to the administrative levels of urban, state and national administration. This configuration requires data and information on whole groups of actors (retailers, consumers, producers, etc.). Although document research has been conducted to gather general information on the retail, food and energy sector in India, it was necessary to collect primary data. Surveys and expert interviews on Kirana shops and electricity consumption in Hyderabad have been conducted in March, April and May 2009. The study on Kirana retailers included structured and semi-structured surveys, which accounted for the groups of consumers, suppliers and supermarkets as they are assessed to have essential (depending, mutual or countervailing) relations to Kirana shops. These groups are as well assumed to become stakeholders within the project on cooperative associations of Kirana shops later on. Concerning the energy consumer study structured interviews and case studies were conducted with private households, commercial units and small-scale industrial establishments. The study reveals a general willingness to cooperate in electricity provision and maintenance and hence lets the selected consumers qualify as primary stakeholders. Expert interviews helped to localise further secondary and potential stakeholders regarding the intended cooperative associations of Kirana shops as well as the intended cooperative association of energy consumers. Overall, both studies provide a basis for further stakeholder integration. Like the primary stakeholders, Kirana shops and energy consumers, the secondary and potential stakeholders (e.g. suppliers and food consumers) are no single actors but groups that encompass diversities of actors. Only subsets of actors within each group will be incorporated when the cooperative associations are formed.

The local focus of the cooperative approach and the concentration of the intended cooperative association on the primary stakeholders, the Kirana shops and energy consumers, have implications for the categorisation of stakeholders, too. The categories for analysis used in other stakeholder analyses like "Organisational Structure" do not have the same relevance in this project. Rather other categories like the "Relation to the Primary Stakeholder" or the "Role in the Intended Association" become important. The intended cooperative associations will promote the primary stakeholders along with certain secondary stakeholders. This promotion countervails the interests of specific further stakeholders. The intended establishment of Kirana associations will for example countervail the interests of supermarkets who stand in a competitive relationship to the traditional retailers. The stakeholder analysis in the field of cooperative self-governance approach has to detect and focus on these relationships. In regard to Kirana associations the description of relations within the stakeholder analysis is especially important as traditional retail relies on a long and diverse supply chain, which has to be accounted for in the cooperative associations later on. Potential and affected stakeholders that are included in the stakeholder analysis in the retail sector are supermarkets (assessed as opponents), wholesalers, suppliers, processors, producers, farmers and consumers who could even be directly incorporated into the cooperative associations later on and change their status from secondary to primary stakeholders along the project. Next to these affected and potentially affecting stakeholders come several governmental stakeholders with monitoring and licensing power in the field of retail and cooperatives and certain additional partners of the project which consult and are involved in designing the cooperative associations. When taking a closer look at energy consumption cooperatives, a similar picture emerges. While the target group for the cooperative associations–private households, commercial units and small scale industrial establishments–as the primary stakeholders stand in the focus of the stakeholder analysis, secondary, potential and governmental stakeholders play a crucial role in the preparation, promotion and implementation processes. First, secondary stakeholders like private companies and NGOs, are indispensible for the practical and technical operation of the cooperative associations. Second, governmental stakeholders not only provide the jurisdictional platform but also may aid with subsidies or further support. Third, it is necessary to collaborate with related associations like Residents Welfare Associations as they bring in local knowledge and act as a starting point for the implementation.

3.3 Stakeholders for institutional and governance changes

The society as a whole and the diversity of households within the lifestyles approach has been covered, as well as small-scale enterprises and households for the cooperative approach. The main formal organisations within the energy sector and their governance structures are covered in the third approach focusing on institutions and governance structures. We have identified a broad set of stakeholders through sampling and grouping exercises as well as an analysis of physical transactions involved in energy provision.

We developed a framework including six basic questions for the analysis of each stakeholder. In addition to (1) the type of stakeholder, we analysed (2) the objectives and interests, (3) the organisational structure, (4) the power and resources, (5) the integration into the stakeholder network and (6) the relation to the project. We drew from a variety of information sources including websites, acts and orders, media, scientific publications, as well as expert interviews conducted in February and March 2009. Together with developing these stakeholder profiles, a categorisation into project partners and primary and secondary stakeholders has been made. In order to reduce complexity, we only focused on the electricity sector (Kimmich et al. 2009). Having set up the stakeholder profiles, we conducted a stakeholder mapping[9] that resembles the one drawn for the lifestyle approach (see Figure 2).

The first participation planning based on the stakeholder map has to be formalised in later project stages. For this formalisation, the tool of a participation-planning matrix as depicted in Figure 3 has been chosen (Bryson 2004: 33). The project consists of a spectrum of tools and methods that have been proposed to develop mitigation and adaptation strategies and are represented in the columns.

Stakeholder / Partner	DPP	CB	SDF	PAP	UEM	EMP	...
TERI	Col	Col	Col	Col	Col	Col	
ECM	Col	Col	Inv	Con	Con	?	
...	?	?	?	?	?		

TERI: The Energy and Resources Institute; ECM: Energy Conservation Mission; DPP: Demonstration and Pilot Projects; CB: Capacity Building; SDF: Sustainable Development Framework; PAP: Perspective Action Plan; UEM: Urban Energy Management Plan; EMP: Energy Master Plan; Col/Inv/Con: see abbreviations in Table 1

Figure 3: Participation planning matrix for project components

Source: Own figure

---

[9] As mentioned above, networks of stakeholders with formal and informal relationships have become increasingly important. This is the case for complex interrelated fields like climate change and the energy sector. Given the broad range of stakeholders that are involved and interact, only concerted actions can induce change in the field. Networks that include private and public organisations are a prominent example, such as the case of a proposed partnership for the production of Renewable Compressed Natural Gas (CNG) in Hyderabad Seshu et al. 2007.

Within the matrix, each stakeholder is related to the project components. The cell indicates the type and means of participation as described in Table 1:

Table 1: Means of participation

Type of participation	Means of participation
Inform (Inf)	To be kept informed about the process
Consult (Con)	To be kept informed, to be consulted and given feedback on how the input influenced the process
Involve (Inv)	To ensure concerns are considered and reflected and given feedback on how the input influenced the process
Collaborate (Col)	To incorporate advices and recommendations to the maximum extent possible
Empower (Emp)	To implement all decisions

Source: based on the participation planning matrix (Bryson 2004: 33)

Each project component requires the participation of a different composition and coalition of stakeholders. The search, development and execution of demonstration projects certainly each need another spectrum of stakeholders to be involved than the development of the Energy Master Plan or capacity building processes. The participation planning process is still in a premature stage. The given participation planning matrix still consists of many question marks. The questions regarding who has to be informed, consulted or involved and with whom collaboration has to be set up at which stage within the process and for what project component has to be decided collectively and repetitively at several stages of the project deployment.

4 Synthesis and conclusions

This paper overviewed methods in stakeholder analyses and exemplified the discussed approaches. We thereby argued that a comprehensive stakeholder analysis at the beginning of any project is crucial for all successive steps up to the implementation phase and hence for the success of a project. A special emphasis was put on the applicability of different methods. We showed that there are several options for conducting stakeholder analyses. Selecting the appropriate stakeholder analysis method depends on the nature of the project. We gave three examples, namely the lifestyle, cooperative and institutional approach, out of an R&D project conducted in Hyderabad. Although we restricted the examples to only the main findings, it became obvious that necessarily different methods were applied. While the cooperative approach found the primary stakeholders in potential members of the aspired cooperative associations, the institutional approach considered rather influential organisations and decision makers as primary stakeholders. Additionally, the identification of the stakeholders requires different methods. Gathering information about potential cooperative's members is most promising via structured questionnaires or interviews. For the institutional approach, research on secondary literature and internet sites followed by expert interviews is more advisable.

We also emphasised the fact that a stakeholder analysis is far more than just a listing of relevant individuals and organisations. It comprises different tools to evaluate and classify stakeholders and compare their influence, power, knowledge and interest within the project and among each other. Our examples showed the stepwise integration of appropriate tools for a meaningful interpretation and evaluation with regard to the objectives of the project. A complete analysis at the outset is hardly possible due to uncertainties that may require a revision of the focus and strategies. Later on, the stakeholder analysis can be an important base for further research on the institutional aspects and governance structures. The action arenas (see e.g. Ostrom 2005) where institutional change takes place, can easily be identified together with the relevant participating stakeholders.

The emphasis on visualisation of the stakeholder analysis process in this study was conducted in order to promote stakeholder participation in the future. Regarding the next steps of the project, the stakeholder maps and diagrams are a good starting point to discuss and amend stakeholder positions and relations in concert with local experts and primary and secondary stakeholders. Only together with these stakeholders is it possible to propose and plan their potential role and contributions to the project. The participation planning diagram highlights certain roles and contributions of identified key stakeholders, but—intentionally—only on the surface. In an intercultural context and given the complexity of a multilayered, emerging megacity, only through stakeholder participation is it feasible to (a) formulate problems adequately and (b) to create ideas for locally adjusted strategic interventions. Both have to be developed through the process of stakeholder interaction in well planned, concerted workshops and sessions in Hyderabad—and, above all, by planning, organising and evaluating concrete demonstration and pilot projects. This will also connect and empower key stakeholders with high interest in the projects' objectives, but little power ('subjects') to exert their influence. In sum, the main benefit for the researchers gained from the stakeholder analysis process is the learning from the stakeholders about local conditions, problems, local institutions and constraints, actors' relationships, power relations and most important, locally developed and adjusted solutions.

References

ASCI. 2005. *City Development Strategy - Hyderabad.* Stakeholder Analysis. Hyderabad.

Bryson, John M. 2004. "What to do when Stakeholders matter." *Public Management Review* 6(1): 21–53.

Eden, Colin, and Fran Ackermann. 1998. *Making strategy. The journey of strategic management.* London etc.: Sage Publications.

Freeman, R. Edward. 1984. *Strategic management. A stakeholder approach.* Boston, Mass.: Pitman.

Grimble, Robin, and Kate Wellard. 1997. "Stakeholder methodologies in natural resource management: a review of principles, contexts, experiences and opportunities. Socio-economic Methods in Renewable Natural Resources Research." *Agricultural Systems,* 55(2): 173–193.

Hagedorn, Konrad. 2008. "Particular requirements for institutional analysis in nature-related sectors." *Eur Rev Agric Econ,* 35(3): 357–384.

Hagedorn, Konrad, Katja Arzt, and Ursula Peters. 2002. "Institutional Arrangements for Environmental Co-operatives: A Conceptual Framework." In *Environmental Co-operation and Institutional Change: Theories and Policies for European Agriculture.* Konrad Hagedorn (ed.). Cheltenham, UK: Edward Elgar.

Hanisch, Markus, Jennifer Meyer-Ueding, and Julian Sagebiel. 2009. "In Search of Low-Emission Pathways: Document and Stakeholder Analysis on Kirana Retailers and Energy Consumers and Background Study on Kirana Retailers." unpublished. Berlin.

Jepsen, Anna L., and Pernille Eskerod. 2009. "Stakeholder analysis in projects: Challenges in using current guidelines in the real world." *International Journal of Project Management,* 27(4): 335–343.

Kimmich, Christian, Hannah Janetschek, and Kai Rommel. 2009. "The Energy Sector in Andhra Pradesh and Hyderabad. A Stakeholder Analysis." unpublished. Berlin.

Mitchell, Ronald K., Bradley R. Agle, and Donna J. Wood. Oct., 1997. "Toward a Theory of Stakeholder Identification and Salience: Defining the Principle of Who and What Really Counts." *The Academy of Management Review,* 22(4): 853–886.

Nutt, Paul C., and Robert W. Backoff. 1992. *Strategic management of public and third sector organizations. A handbook for leaders.* San Francisco: Jossey-Bass Publishers.

Ostrom, Elinor. 2005. *Understanding institutional diversity*. Princeton, Oxford: Princeton University Press.

Powell, Walter W. "Neither market nor hierarchy: network forms of organization." In *Markets, hierarchies and networks. The coordination of social life*. G. Thompson (ed.). London: SAGE.

Reed, Mark S., Anil Graves, Norman Dandy, Helena Posthumus, Klaus Hubacek, Joe Morris, Christina Prell, Claire H. Quinn, and Lindsay C. Stringer. 2009. "Who's in and why? A typology of stakeholder analysis methods for natural resource management." *Journal of Environmental Management*, 90(5): 1933–1949.

Reusswig, Fritz, H. Lotze-Campen, and K. Gerlinger. 2003. "Changing global lifestyle and consumption patterns: the case of energy and food." Paper presented at the *PERN Workshop on Population, Consumption, and Environment Dynamics: theory and method*. Montréal.

Reusswig, Fritz, Lutz Meyer-Ohlendorf, and Ulrike Anders. 2009a. "Partners for a Low-Carbon Hyderabad - A Stakeholder Analysis with respect to "Lifestyle Dynamics and Climate Change." unpublished. Potsdam.

Reusswig, Fritz, Antje Otto, Lutz Meyer-Ohlendorf, and Ulrike Anders. 2009b. "Climate Change Discourse in India: An Analysis of Press Articles." unpublished. Potsdam.

Seshu, Rama, Shashi Kumar, Vinod Iyengar, Vittal Gudavalli, Usha Gour, Saibal Guha, Saugat Mukherjee, and K. P. Singh. 2007. "Public Private Partnership in Hyderabad. A Feasibility Study on Proposed PPP on Renewable Compressed Natural Gas (CNG) Production from Sewerage Treatment." Berlin; Hyderabad.

Sudarshan, Anant. 2008. "Lifestyles, energy consumption, and climate change: a global view of the links." *Energy Security Insights*, 2: 2–9.